you don't like basketball?

You don't like camping?

So if you don't like

any

of that stuff, what do you like?

Hi! I'm Jevon and a lot of people make fun of me because I don't like the same things that other kids my age like.

I don't know why I am not good at sports, or why I don't like learning about cars, or why I don't like to sleep outside at night.

I don't know why I don't have a need to sit on the couch and watch TV, play on my phone, or play video games all day.

I don't know why I don't have a need, want, or urge to throw a wire into the lake and see if I can catch a fish.

I don't know why I don't have a need, want, or urge to use a hammer, power tools or a measuring tape.

I don't know why

I don't know why

I like
drawing and painting.

I don't know why

I like reading lots of books.

I don't know why

I like studying insects.

I don't know why

I like learning about plants.

I don't know why

I like playing chess.

I don't know why

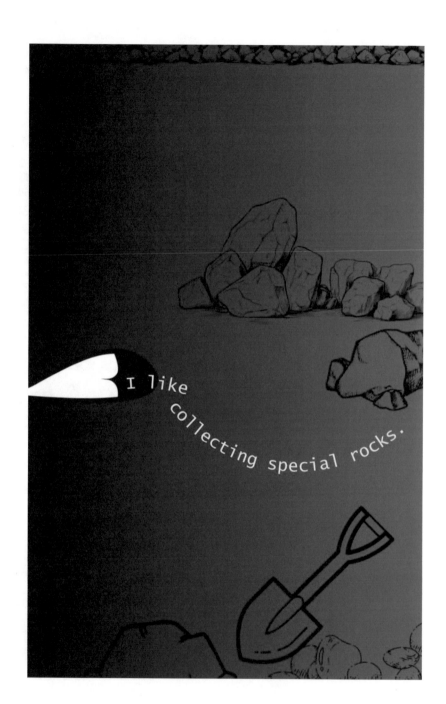

I like collecting special rocks.

I don't know why

I like surfing.

I don't know why

I don't know why

I don't know why

I don't know why

I like volunteering.

VOLUNTEERS *NEEDED*

I don't know why I like to do the things that I like to do, but when I do them I feel happy.

It makes me happy

when I hang out with my friends.

It makes me happy

when I buy a new outfit.

It makes me happy

It makes me happy

when I do good in school.

Those are the things that make me happy. These are the things that I think are cool.

Its cool when

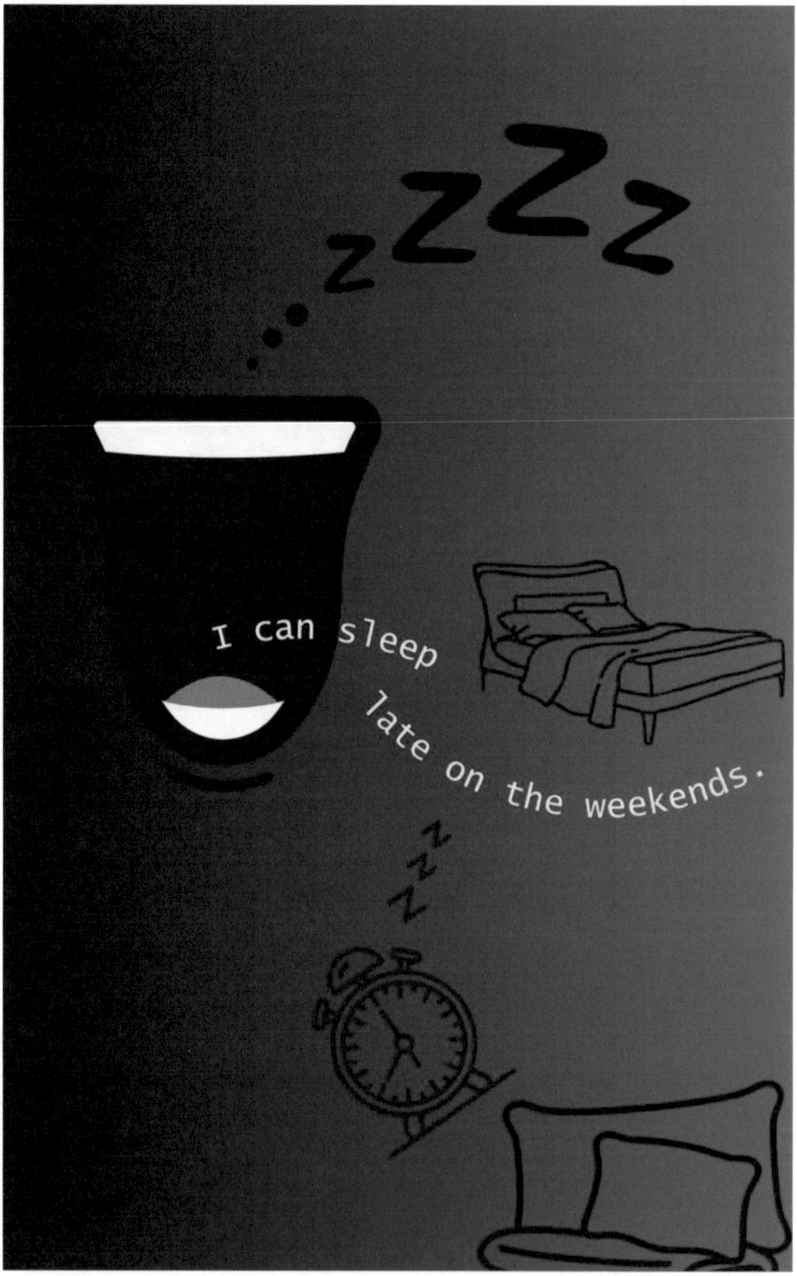
zZZz
I can sleep
late on the weekends.

Its cool when

I earn money for doing chores.

Its cool when

I watch
movies with my family.

Its cool when

I get to go on vacations.

Its cool when

I ride amusement park rides.

Its cool when

I stand up for what I believe in.

SPEAK UP

Its cool when

I don't give into peer pressure.

Its cool when

But most importantly....

Its cool when

Made in the USA
Columbia, SC
16 February 2025